Mind's Eye Musings

Thomas Raher

For my wife Christine who thinks I've taken blah, blah, blah to a new level, and my sons Ramsey, Cassidy and Brendan who I hope some of the blah, blah has rubbed off on!

Preface

I've always wanted to write a memoir. Leading up to such an endeavor I've practiced by keeping journals, writing and saving letters. and more recently creating a blog site. These writing tasks have been going on for over forty years. I have a garage full of journal notebooks with daily entries as sparse as the miles I ran or the food I ate. Hardly worth compiling yet available for the archives. My blog site became a more elaborate journal with much fewer entries, but entries expressing more. This blog has been going on for about ten years, coinciding with the digital movement. Here I sit trying, while procrastinating, to piece the puzzle of my life's memories together, and figured I might as well compile my blog postings. It's a matter of vanity and wanting to be remembered. I'll be gone soon enough and if I never finish the big story, at least there will be these snippets for my loved ones to mull over.

**I want to be buried in an anonymous crater inside the moon.
I want to prove that the sun was born when God fell asleep
with a lit cigarette,
tired after a hard night of judging.
I want to prove once and for all I'm not crazy.**

~ Bob Kaufman

A s you can see the year is drawing to a close. I'm listening to my last Christmas CD, *A Jazzy Christmas*, with the likes of Dinah Washington, Billie Holiday and Peggy Lee. The season has taken its toll as it does each year. All the preparations and plans can and usually do come unglued. This year just as the family came together we were struck down by the pernicious and ubiquitous flu bug. We had to apply the covid protocols and separate individuals from the family herd to control the contagion. Unfortunately we were second to fall victim to the sickness, consequently we were eliminated from certain fun family functions. These new viruses tend to linger much longer than expected. Physically and mentally they are draining, which is frustrating, because you can't join in the festive fray without worrying about spreading the flu. We did the best we could and survived full of joy and blessings for the optimum minutes we did share.

If the ongoing news is any indicator we were the lucky ones. At least we were home, the millions traveling to be with friends and relatives were met with unbelievable obstacles. Blizzards, ice, whiteouts, airline cancellations, all of epic proportions stranded million across the land. Extreme seems to be the new common. The holidays are supposedly a time to remind us what is meaningful. A time for centering. I think mostly it is adjusting. Adjusting to extremes. Adjusting our momentum from fast to slow. Adjusting our audio from chatter to listening. One aspect of being under the weather is the silence in isolation. Sickness force adjustments, concentration, reflection, quiet, stillness, a kind of meditation or medication. Adjusting.

A new year is just around the corner and adjusting will be a primary ingredient. You see I've gotten old and my body forces constant and permanent adjustments. I'm learning tolerance by having to tolerate all the things I can no longer do. This is extreme because all my life I took for granted certain abilities would last. But now the obvious limitations need tolerance and adjusting. As the larger world grows ever more extreme, so does my personal world. Adjusting to the simplest tasks becomes extremely more difficult. And so it goes!

Merry Christmas and Happy New Year!

"I'll see you in the funny papers."

So what? Always the question, to express more opinions, observations, attitudes, ideas, and remembrances or forget about it. Who really cares and do I even care? Sometimes I feel the need to write because somebody might read it and get a sense of who I am or was. But what to write? Current events is always good for ranting and raving, family matters rekindle what is joyous, especially children's development, the increasing aches and pains of aging, comparing the experiences of the past and present, you see just spewing spontaneously writes itself.

The holiday season is in full swing. Halloween just concluded and fortunately I didn't have to participate. I've always been shy and introverted and I am reluctant to dressing in elaborate costumes. I don't mind eating exorbitant amounts of candy but at my age excessive sugar is a killer. Not to mention the excessive nature of the upcoming holidays and the stresses involved. I'm already strategizing the use of aches and pains of old age, as well as old age itself, as a means to minimize holiday activities. We'll see, I've survived this long!

It's been months since I've written for this blog. I sense it becomes repetitive. I find myself most of the time a cynic steeped in fatalism. I have to urge myself to be optimistic and glean the positive and beautiful from the world around me. It's easy with grand children because of their innocence and exuberance. But distance of sorts keeps us apart. So the ongoing pernicious politics of life swarms over my psyche like a cloud of wasps. Our country is torn in two without a bridge of compromise, and a real civil war, with weaponry, festers just below the surface. I fear the gloom and doom!

Then there is getting old. I'm 74 now and realizing begrudgingly I'm basically irrelevant and invisible. I had a revelation yesterday, let go of the ego, and unnecessary expectations. Sounds simple doesn't it. Actually the more alone you or I are the easier it gets. The aches and pains grow and functioning on most physical levels ceases, which eliminates expectations. Since performing socially is curtailed by physical restrictions there's no need for ego. Impressing on any level is unnecessary when you are alone, so who needs an ego. This awareness although difficult is relieving.

A man is just about as happy as he makes up his mind to be!

8/4/22

I'm in isolation. Finally after two years of conscious caution I've been waylaid by the persistent Covid virus. I turned 74 on July 28 and boy does that sound old. What happened was I saw an ad for a Tommy Castro and the Painkillers show. My youthful exuberance surged and I dug deeper. The band was playing on my birthday at the SF Jazz Center which was a natural inducement, because the venue is down at the Civic Center and just a 5 Fulton bus ride away. Anyway it was a special night full of great music and I got to reconnect with an old friend, the base player, Randy MacDonald. I'm building here. A couple days before that outing another extravaganza took place. Our San Francisco Lawn Bowling Club was honoring our oldest member. Arnie Barros was turning 100, truly phenomenal. The festivities included bowling in the morning and a catered lunch of Arnie's choice. Our district supervisor proclaimed it Arnie's Day with a framed City Hall certificate. Of course our club President made a speech extolling Arnie's long history of achievements, while Arnie sat smiling and eating. Over a hundred of Arnie's admirers including a huge contingent of his extended family, were on hand for this monumental occasion. There's more. A day after my birthday I had been scheduled by my dear wife Christine to help, as she hosted her cousins. Again we utilized the bowling club because her traveling clan was thirteen strong. They are from the Midwest and were obliged to visit all the favorite SF tourist attractions. They weren't wearing masks and by the way masks were optional in all of these large social gatherings. They had a good time and Christine instructed them on the basics of bowling and provided snacks making for a comfortable afternoon. It was a short visit because they had to race to Pier 39 to catch a tour boat circling the bay before leaving for Fresno. Whirlwind. So for a guy who has avoided social contact pretty much throughout this pandemic, I virtually jumped into the deep end. The day after the cousins left the virus symptoms surfaced all together.

The symptoms seem to be waning but I still tested positive this morning. I'm watching the Giants and Dodgers on my iPhone while I update my blog on my laptop. Lucky me I have all I need and I made 74 who'd a thunk. I guess I'll see ya in the funny papers!

Today the battle rages between external and internal forces. The difficulty is keeping them separate. They overlap and mingle so as to upset the balance. My very precarious mental balance that is. Why is balance necessary? Simply because it minimizes stress and we all know stress kills. Most all of society's ills, maladies, ailments, dysfunction, are totally or partially attributed to stress. Stress rears its ugliness in myriad and varied ways. Everything we think or do has an element of stress. But if we can limit the stress by separating the external, jobs, finance, wars, politics, traffic, with the internal, anxiety, regret, self esteem, fear, well just maybe the battle isn't a total loss.

Solitude can play an important role and something I've decided to utilize more and more. It's easier to control the environment when you are alone and quiet. You needn't allow the external stress to invade your privacy, your solitude. Then the internal stress of your own making can be dealt with calmly and peacefully. Separate and balance. I found as I get older I need less and less. I've also found when out and about interacting socially the external stress, even the happy stress of family gatherings, manifests itself physically. Nerve endings react, pimples/bumps, tooth-aches, rashes/hives, muscle and joint aches, and occur for no apparent reason. Stress.

You see if I want my quality of life, which is certainly limited as I approach 74 years old, to be joyful, then I must adjust to these new realities. I know it's difficult for friends and family, who only know the persona I've cultivated over a lifetime, to wonder what's the matter. I can't go around trying to explain that I'm adapting to the mental and physical person I've become. Although I do and those explanations seem futile and or inadequate, which is more stress. So you see I'm leaning more and more toward solitude however much the external forces tug at me to get out there.

I desire to live in peace and to continue the life I have begun under the motto "to live well you must live unseen." ~ Rene Descartes

The human race exaggerates everything: its heroes, its enemies, its importance. ~ Charles Bukowski

Blessed be he who has found his solitude, not the solitude pictured in painting or poetry, but his own, unique, predestined solitude. Blessed be he who knows how to suffer! To him comes destiny, from him comes authentic action. ~ Hermann Hesse

A few quotes from mental friends, I hope you don't mind.

T oday is Mardi Gras, Fat Tuesday, the eve of Lent. We are still in the throes of the Covid epidemic but much less so. Most people have been vaccinated and hospitals report fewer cases and less emergency over crowding. Restrictions on mask wearing mandates are being lifted and a cautious normalcy is returning. Let the good times roll and let's celebrate Fat Tuesday in true tradition before the fasting and abstinence begins tomorrow. I'm also celebrating 16 years of sobriety. There was a time when a planned celebration was in order. Food and drink, colorful beads and hats to match, loud music and raucous behavior, a mighty release, but no more. Those days of revelry are a thing of the past, a distant memory. Not only am I sober but I got old. So staying sober is hardly a challenge, because I do very little of anything. Although when I look around this very polarized world, autocrats vs democrats, authoritarians vs egalitarians, it makes me sad and frustrated, and God knows I could use a strong drink. The human fabric gets more frayed and chaotic as remedies and solutions seem impossible. I hunker down in my solitude and wait patiently for the grandchildren, in their innocence and exuberance to fish me out of my mental quagmire. Being with them and their skipping and smiles and robust parading around, makes each minute a Mardi Gras. Their unencumbered hopeful joy is a much a needed balancer, juxtaposed against the great expanse of despair for far too many.

I reflect on my own youth when adult problems were yet to come. Like my grandkids I played with abandon, all day if I could. I would get weary from the sheer joy exhausting all my energy. I was comfortable and confident in my own skin and my family environment. I was happy and growing and learning and absorbing. I was a sponge filling with happy and exciting experiences. I'm reminded of that long ago life when I'm with the children and I feel good. But like that long ago idyllic life, change happens and we can't and don't stay children. The adult world, the world of suffering, the world of injustice, the world of hopelessness, encroaches my consciousness.

I'll celebrate Mardi Gras sober, with my children and their children on my mind, and all the joy they've brought me in my life, and give thanks.

12/22/21

I guess you could say winter has arrived. The temperature has been in the forties. The weather casters are no longer singing the fearful drought refrain. Real rain storms have continued saturating our thirsty land and dumping tons of snow in the mountains. All good for our future water needs. The grey wet days with glistening streets and reflecting rain drops add to the spirit of the holiday season. Christmas is just a few short days away. The weather keeps us indoors with the thermostat turned up, and the darker, shorter days allows for turning on all the colorful Christmas lights. Ambiance is the key to holiday cheer. Instrumental Christmas carols provide background music, while the muted television shows irrelevant football bowl games and myriad college basketball games. Tamales are steaming on the stove. Reminisces are the main subject of conversation and thumbing through old photo albums. Where are the children now? Happily with their own children!

Unfortunately we all can't gather to share our lifetime of experiences. Distance is one culprit. The Covid virus in all its mutations continues to surge and the latest version is more transmissible. It's been nearly two years and the social restrictions, which had eased are now back in place. Isolation is once again in play. So although we have all the external manifestations of a wonderful Christmas, the deadly virus hangs over our collective cheer like Scrooge himself! But the spirit is indomitable and we are secure in our comforting devices, like rum balls, eggnog, chocolate truffles, mint candy, assorted nuts of which we are included, old classic movies we've memorized over the years, and good books when there is a lull. And we can give our time and money, what little we have, where we think it helps. Close to home in most cases, and remembering to extend an open hand of tolerance, to paraphrase a concluding line in one of my favorite movies, *The Bishop's Wife*!

I don't have many Christmases left. I won't be dwelling on the usual negativities I have no control over. I'd usually list them here, but I'm sure you know what they are. Anyway in my old age I'm attempting to create a better balance and rid the useless negativity from my battling psychos. On that note I want to wish a Merry Christmas to all and to all a good night.

Here's a few family photos of this year dedicated to our loved ones long gone!

11/19/21

---

oday I finished a pseudo biography of Lawrence Ferlinghetti. It's
incredible. He recounted his youth somewhat, but mostly it was a
stream of conscious illumination. We shared his journey through Greek
mythology, iconic philosophers, beat poets, American politics, the digital
age, business as usual, and social injustice. It's an amazing rant, a brilliant
rant on materialism, capitalism, spirituality, religion, climate change and
our ultimate demise. I was enthralled because he elucidates with humor
and clarity all the ills of a society at perpetual crossroads. I envy his ability
to rattle off these complexities, their essence, and expose them for debate.
He speaks to me and says what I would if I could. I concluded reading it
this morning and the last line was, "AND that is why the cries of birds now
are not cries of ecstasy but cries of despair.'

As I closed my eyes to ponder and absorb what I just read, my wife
interrupted my reverie informing me a young murderer, symbolic of our
extremist home grown terrorists, had been acquitted. This form of right
wing vigilantism steeped in racism no longer fears repercussions. The law,
a term I use lightly because it doesn't work for all, has become absurd.
White rage, white backlash, white power has been reinforced, and
validated by a radicalized judicial system. It's only getting worse. Our
government is torn in two and doesn't work, our society is torn in two and
there's no overlap, violence in all its many forms seems to be the only
recourse. We are killing ourselves and we are killing our planet, not at all a
rosy picture. Worst of all my golf game has deteriorated to have become
boring and no fun!

See ya in the funny papers. 😎

___

his blog is a personal rant. I only bother to write it because I know it probably won't be read. You see yesterday my son sent a golf video of me six years ago titled Veterans Day. I made an assumption mistakenly. A bit of a back story is in order. First I have three sons which makes for the ideal dream golfing foursome. I'm a veteran (Army) and my oldest son is a veteran (Army). He by the way has two Purple Hearts, seeing action in both Iraq and Afghanistan. A few years ago good fortune conspired and we all came together on Veterans Day for a family round of golf. It was a success and we decided a tradition was born. Last year of course the Pandemic put the kibosh on our convergence. Now though public gatherings aren't as restrictive. So when I received my son's message with the video earmarked Vets Day, I thought he was reaching out and planning our traditional golf outing. I messaged back about what's what. Now comes the shock. He said his brother, my son, was coming from Portland specifically for golf, and he had notified my other son, which makes three. Here it comes. Then he says he penciled in his cousin, my nephew as the fourth, and I'd be sitting this one out. I was stunned, shunned, snubbed and dissed.

What hurt and cut to the bone was my failure to realize they didn't share my sensibility about this family event. You see it should be a poignant and singular chance to acknowledge our four generations of Vets, and all Vets. Plus the lads have their own families and live in different locales, meaning once a year the four of us could be together, for a half day, without the responsibility and distractions of women and children. Alone, sharing laughter, reminiscing, reinforcing our bonds. When the boys were little I fantasized about a family foursome when they were all adults. Back then I got them clubs, showed them the fundamentals, watched them get better and grow to love the game. My dream foursome had come true.

I got old. I suppose now I don't measure up. It's a hard reality to accept. I'm no longer an integral ingredient in a foursome I thought would last. I don't begrudge the boys, I've never let expectations rule.

~ Shattered Toe

I haven't written a word in a good long time. Why? Ideas, opinions, declarations, all seem irrelevant. The problem it seems is containment. The overlap of personal dilemmas and national political dilemmas is a matter to be resolved. How? Deciphering and analyzing the problems and studying a possible solution. Ironically this mission is similar. Measuring for what enhances one's existence and that which doesn't. What then from each quandary can I contain and nurture? The big picture of a national government stymied by intransigence without any sense of compromise is utterly frustrating. I've decided to disassociate myself from the daily news cycle because it overwhelmingly detracts from any personal enhancement. The political divide and utter polarization sucks the positivity out of the air. It's difficult enough inhaling and exhaling the constant air of greed, corruption and deceit, so I tune out.

Now closer to home tuning out would have the opposite effect. It's about balance. The negative affect from the macro-view of an incompetent government is balanced positively by multiple micro-spheres. Foremost is family. After a long lifetime of suffering the observance of injustice and inequality, children old and new are the ultimate saving grace. When I'm slumping near depression I can bask in the happy, humorous, innocent laughter of children and grandchildren. There's nothing quite as powerful as the unconditional love of a toddler grinning at the very sight of you. They want to be needed and the need to be wanted. Existence enhancers. Extending beyond the family are small social circles built around positive and uplifting activities. Friends who reinforce what is good and are civil, shining examples of what could be. Understanding and containing what only enhances our lives and understanding and ridding what detracts from a graceful view. The balancing act is necessary for peace of mind. Mindfulness!

05/06/21

Today is another unremarkable day. I did feel the need to post something, anything on my blog. I guess I should start with what's happening with the Covid-19 pandemic. Now that the radical trump administration has been more or less deleted, the government under Biden's guidance can get busy. Nearly two thirds of the adult population has been vaccinated and the production and distribution is moving forward. Reported cases continue to drop as well as deaths and hospitals can breathe a bit easier. Certain restrictions have been lifted and businesses are starting to open. People can gather in ever larger groups, like sporting events, and masks are less mandatory. All in all people are still cautious but less fearful, as a sense of normalcy creeps slowly back. The country is still unalterably divided though and the fabric of America is torn. The future is one big bold question mark. I choose the here and now.

Maybe I'll just complain about every little thing like most old codgers. Those complaints center around the inevitable deterioration of the body, which keeps me definitely in the now. Different levels of pain are evenly spread throughout most joints and muscles. Any movement takes focus because you never know how the body will react or not act. I was trying to carry heavy grocery bags up the stairs. First I lifted one to make sure my back could do the job. Then I put one in each hand and lifted insuring my biceps and elbow joints were up to the task. All this before taking a step. The climb up the stairs is the real test. Now that the upper body seems able, the first step up will indicate how competent the lower half is. The aching hip, knee and atrophying thigh muscle all cry out, stop! Fortunately they push the weight upward, but one bag is heavier and the process begins to tilt, and I stop to regain balance and catch my breath.

Focus. Up I go finally getting to the kitchen and start unpacking. I used to take all these body movements for granted. Now each action is calculated. This focused calculation keeps me cemented in the now. Sometimes I stay still avoiding action and pain, which also keeps me in the now. Oh well, cliché..."nobody said it would be easy."

Thinking on...my son springs to mind. He's experiencing aging and has been struggling and learning about the now. And I'm happy to report his dedication and focus are exemplary. Happiness is elusive and illusionary when searching afar. But when you realize playing with and teaching your son in the very now, you begin to understand happiness. Which I think he has. When I see the laughter and interaction displayed when they are together my heart soars. His now is my now! Love...

02/19/21

The relationship between age, or old age, and current events, the strange and difficult times we are living through, at least I am, is perplexing to say the least. A half a million Americans have died of the Covid virus. Seniors are the most vulnerable but now they are first to receive vaccines. I've received the first of two vaccine shots and feel somewhat relieved. But we are by no means anywhere near normalcy. Schools are closed and teachers are fearful, and shouldn't they be first to be vaccinated. Businesses are struggling mightily to stay alive. Jobs are scarce and the economy is suffering. Legislators remain stymied by intransigence to provide financial help for all. It's been a long and tumultuous year with many levels of anxiety. The new year and new administration have provided a much needed hope however illusory.

I zoomed with my granddaughter last evening, a treat, I'm watching golf on TV thinking I should exercise, as life marches on. My point is the fragile conditions for most don't really affect me. Being old I'm concerned about climate change, but only in regards to my grandchildren because I'll be long gone from this world. Since I'm retired with a secure pension and social security, the financial woes affecting the average American aren't a worry. In a self-centered way I smirk at the obvious travails burdening most. Only for a moment. I do really feel a deep sorrow, a sadness for my fellow humans affected through no fault of their own. Our democratic system, which we have taken for granted, has been threatened and come under question. All the problems and struggles we face seem less for me simply because of my age. As I near the end of this remarkable journey I linger on all I've been gifted. Needless worry is just that, and I don't have time for it.

The larger problems of the world dwindle after my coffee takes effect. I cross my legs and stare out into the misty morning. My worry shifts. Will that lady quiet her yapping dog, which is driving me bonkers. Are the neighbor kids playing in the fairy garden going to be nice or destroy? Is my neighbor in the upstairs flat going to use the washer and dryer all day or what? Do I have to remind Christine, who's at the grocery store, not to forget the peanut butter? Am I going to have to go outside and help the nervous driver trying to parallel park? These are my kind of problems, which I personally can deal with if I choose. Ice bergs melting, global virus threats, republican insurrection, however worrisome are out of my league.

I really have nothing to add, the twenty-four hour story tellers and pseudo pundits continuously inundate us with speculation and bias ad nauseam. So I'll bid you adieu until another blog update.

01/04/21

A full moon shone brightly ushering in the new year. I wish the change I and we need occurred spontaneously with the calendar page flip. But it won't happen. Democracy is still teetering as Trump refuses to concede his election loss. He is a tiresome individual and his lies are so tedious yet half of all Americans believe and support him. Go figure. I guess they'll have to drag him screaming from the Oval Office!

Since Thanksgiving, when millions defied stay home recommendations, the covid virus has surged and spread. Hospitals are at capacity. The numbers are staggering but vaccines have been produced and distributed. Time will tell how successful the vaccines are even with new strains of the virus emerging. Politics and the virus are waiting games coated in speculation and doubt. It certainly has been a tumultuous and fretful year, but there is a glimmer of hope for the future.

Although major gatherings were replaced by FaceTime and individual family visits, the Christmas holiday worked just fine. The necessary precautions were taken, masks were worn as needed and outdoor visits minimized questionable contact. Gifts were exchanged, food shared and enjoyed keeping the holiday spirit as close to traditional as possible. Christine had our humble abode decked out in shimmering Christmas splendor. Colored lights warmed each room and heirloom ornaments decorated our view with memories of past joy.

So you see as the world fluctuates ever precariously between levels of chaos, we manage to maintain our pride of spirit sharing traditions of goodwill and tolerance. So I'll conclude this brief blog post with a couple of recent notes, one a haiku the other a wish!

Change happens simply
By stepping across time lines
Puzzling but hopeful

May your walls know joy,
may every room hold laughter,
and every window open to great possibility.
Happy New Year!

11/02/20

Well now, the summer has come and gone, but the Coronavirus is still with us and surging. Who thought this scourge couldn't be contained. Unfortunately there is no national leadership mandating the necessary safeguards to limit the spread. So we wait impatiently for big pharma to produce a vaccine. The waiting game continues with people eschewing guidelines risking the fate of themselves and the public. All this dominating the public's attention as the absurd presidential race comes to a merciful conclusion. Tomorrow, Nov. 3 we vote. Frankly our democracy is at stake. Will the absurd incumbent, spewing lies, derision, racism, unbridled authoritarianism, win and advance the plutocracy. Or his opponent trying to unite the people around basic notions of compassion and inclusion. Tomorrow will tell the tale!

The months long pandemic, with no end in sight, raised awareness for me on many fronts. How to interact with family and friends from a distance for example. Actions had to be thought out, planned and executed accordingly. Spontaneity took a back seat and rightly so. Most group actions were simply eliminated altogether. And as the holiday season rapidly approaches traditional gatherings will be rethought. It has been a difficult time but our collective resilience shines through. Children miss school, adults miss partying, money for most is a problem, unhealthy politics rolls on, yet humor emerges from all the misery. We are generally a hopeful lot. For folks my age, well we've seen society come unraveled more than a few times. However despairing each upheaval, it passed. Emotional devastation and heartbreak, whether from without or within, will subside eventually, hopefully. Although this trump train has been utterly depressing. And I come from the streets, where our anthem, mantra was "Fuck It." So seven months of growing a beard as a fuck it statement to the pandemic and trump's hypocrisy, took me back to a time when I disdained the establishment with every fiber in my body.

I've been reading many different authors expressing clearly and analytically their thoughts on our time in relation to history. Perspective always reassures the doubter, that's me, and visiting other, brighter, folks' perspectives boosts my morale and off sets my cynicism. In the end, which is coming, when I want to close the door behind me, I turn my frown upside down and carry on. Ciao!

All Souls Day

Peace

07/20/20

I self-published through LULU publishing and LIMELIGHT publishing a compilation of haikus while sheltering in place. It was more a lark and daily exercise but eventually grew. The problem was the virus wasn't ending and I couldn't continue forever. So I stopped and this is what became of my effort.

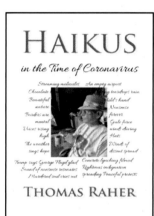

Thomas Raher has written a very insightful book of Haikus, entitled, *HAIKUS in the Time of Coronavirus*.

About the Book: For Thomas Raher, 2020 started with a bang. The beginning of a new decade. Then the Coronavirus turned the world inside out. Using the standard haiku format, he noted everything as he sheltered and stared out the window. Raher utilized this strict structure to express his thoughts simply. Sheltering in place was a means to be creative. He captures the many aspects brought on by the virus. His chronology and metaphors illuminate the big picture affecting us all. Although the time frame was a mere three months, he manages to grasp the seismic shifts in society. This work can be read as staccato prose, or the poetry he intended.

About the Author: Thomas Raher is retired. He was most severely influenced by the "Beats." San Francisco, his home, has a significant role in the who and why of Himself. Although he completed a career as a public servant (transit operator), and helped raised three sons, his mind has always been "on the road."

He has two other publications:

Letters from a Working Stiff (2013) - A composite of writings to family and friends reflecting on the challenges of raising a family, driving a bus, and maintaining an individual sense of identity.

Smiling Eyes - Memories of Youth (2019) - Short stories of youth written to his dying mother.

How to connect with Thomas Raher
Blogspot: tomraher.blogspot.com
Facebook: Thomas Raher (@tomraher1)
Instagram: tomraher1
Twitter: @tomraher1

06/09/20

Sister Susan's Seventieth Birthday.

Pandemic. Virus. Isolation. Sheltering. Police. Murder. Death. Protests. Riots. Looting.

These are the times we live in. Mentally and physically taxing our senses. I have to examine daily the entire gamut of emotions. It's a veritable roller coaster ride. Thrust into this mixing bowl of uncertain ingredients was my sister's birthday.

My brother Casey and I discussed months ago the absolute need to be with her on her 70th birthday. We are now old. A condition unthinkable not so long ago, but here we are. Limitations abound. Unfortunately she is most affected by limitations. She lives below the poverty line in an unforgiving tract of high desert. Stuck. The only redemptive quality is she can dip her toes in the cool Colorado river when temperatures settle at 110 degrees. She's alone. She's suffered ongoing culture shock for the long 25 years she's been in Bullhead City. Hence the importance of our being there.

Casey and I put our heads together trying to form a travel plan. A back story surfaced as a template for such a journey. You see in 1977 Susan was in a difficult situation. She lived in Chicago and her little world had crumbled. Casey and I lived here in San Francisco. She reached out to us for help rescuing her. We didn't hesitate. Casey had a classic Pontiac Catalina convertible road tested and ready to go. We set sail nonstop arriving in the Windy City in 40 hours. She was grateful to see us. The car was loaded, we reversed course and headed due West. A memorable trip!

Initially we planned to load Casey's van with lawn chairs, a cooler, and other amenities for the long 10-hour drive to Arizona. A certain reenactment of that awesome 43-year-old journey of brotherly love. We tried to discount vision problems, bad backs, stiff knees, pot bellies, and other assorted maladies. It would be historic. Lucky for me, his son Drew desired to go which changed the dynamic. He was flying in from Boston on the wrong day at the wrong time. Everything changed. The new timeline wasn't conducive for me. My enthusiasm drained. I even thought of bowing out, but that would be shamefully inexcusable. I needed to honor her long struggle. Frankly the change in plans worked better for me. I flew to Vegas, an hour and a half, rented a car and drove the 90 miles to her house, easy peasy.

I arrived a day ahead of Casey and Drew, which allowed me and Sue time to catch up uninterrupted. I hadn't visited her in probably 10 years. Our hug was deeply felt and emotional, significant because of our age and mortality. She launched into showing me all the detailed work she'd done making ready her humble abode. It was stunning. So much to see and linger over, while listening to the labor involved over the previous month. I commented adoringly it was a 3D mixed media art display on a grand scale. She should charge admission. She talked and talked interspersing reminisces with recent happenings, painting a large splendid picture of her life over time.

The next afternoon the boys rolled in like thunder. Casey drove alone from San Francisco to Las Vegas because Drew changed his plans. To arrive at Sue's a bit earlier, Drew flew to Vegas where Casey picked him up. A long tiring drive for old Casey but he's a good sport. Casey presented the birthday girl a beautiful bouquet, a grand gesture, while Drew hauled the cooler of iced beer out of the van. Once greeted and seated Casey broke out the cigars and the love fest was underway. The joy of being together at last was infectious and laughter reigned or rained.

There were no extravagant plans for her birthday. Just being in each other's presence was the balm needed. We did enjoy a delicious lunch at her favorite local spot, high on a hill overlooking the valley. She had her heart set on a Rueben sandwich with German potato salad, washing it down with a margarita, and wasn't disappointed. When back outside we were gobsmacked by the suffocating heat. Her usual ritual is to submerge herself and a lawn chair in the cold rushing water of the Colorado river, not 500 yards from her front door. Needless to say we all followed for the refreshing dunking. We spent the better part of the day sitting near the shore while the waves lapped up around us neutralizing the stifling heat. Later in the evening as the moon rose and the temperature dropped to 101, we ordered delivery from her favorite Italian restaurant. We enjoyed a leisurely dinner with Spumoni ice cream for dessert. The banter was light and as refreshing as the cool river waters. Old family members remembering childhood, and the experiences that bound us. A much needed stroll down memory lane, ending with genuine hugs of endless love.

Happy Birthday Susan Ellen Raher!!

This black and white photo is from 1977. The scene is the Great Salt Flats. We stopped for a break and a Kodak minute! We were driving from Chicago to San Francisco!

Sunday is under way and before I take a walk and settle in to watch some golf, I want to post a letter I wrote to an old and dear friend. I don't utilize this blog site as much as I'd like, and this is an alternate way.

Sir Tom,

Yeah, old age is definitely a condition we have to adjust to. It's tricky though. For me it's mostly mental. I spend a lot of time weighing the pros and cons, and balancing notions and influences. On one hand senior reports from groups like AARP, local Y's, community centers, all profess social interaction is the panacea. On the other hand ancient prophets and poets remind us solitude and practicing being still, calms the restless soul. I'm inclined to the latter and thoroughly enjoy my aloneness. But when out in public, whether golfing with friends or lawn bowling, I do enjoy the physical aspect and the casual banter. My problem with being social is I see the world as it really is, a hypocritical quagmire of greed and oppression. So engaging in small talk always seems inadequate.

Then I fight to balance the pessimism with some hope. Like this morning I decided to attend Mass with Christine attempting to rekindle an innocent faith in a myth espousing charity and compassion. Long before I became calloused to the machinations of the real world, when I was young altar boy, I glowed in happy hope. A sensation I can barely urge to the surface, a memory long blurred by time. But all of this is part of daily life and I waft in and around all of it constantly.

I just finished a remarkable book, *The Stones of Summer*, by Dow Mossman. He grew up in CR and It's an abstract depiction of his youthful rite of passage. He graduated from the Writers Workshop at Iowa and his book was highly acclaims when it was published in '72. Then he dropped off the face of the earth. But the book has resurfaced and I was fortunate to have been made aware. This is where solitude comes in and spending long periods alone, but not alone. Wandering through the universe of another's mind and finding the similarities and relating totally.

Well buddy, I'm well physically. Just had a physical and all vitals are normal. My liver seems to have rebounded somewhat and all my blood tests are in the proper range. I get 6 to 10 thousand steps in most days, weather permitting. For a guy our age I'm hanging in there. Attitude and tolerance are things to focus on. I have to remember or be conscious of, in a fast paced, youth oriented society, that I'm virtually invisible. All my significant influences and influencers, are unknown and meaningless to the young, especially my grandkids. So being in the now, when I'm with the young, makes me feel like I'm in a lifeboat floating alone far from anything. And all that I know and all that I experienced has disappeared and I wonder why I cling to it. Ah the challenge!

My boys are busy with their lives and doing splendidly, and when I'm with them I try to infuse my introspection, just to see if anyone is listening. Even though we know in the end it doesn't matter!

Peace brother!

I voted for Bernie... fuck Trump and the oligarchy...

01/17/20

2020 looks impressive. It certainly has a fluidity as a time marker. I do have a bit of a problem fixing myself now, in this time. Speaking the number and visualizing my past, in the broader historical picture, confounds. What the number really implies is I'm as old as the hills. When I'm out and about in polite society, of which there is very little, I realize begrudgingly, a good many were only born in this century. Century, another time concept to ponder. But what am I talking about. Time. The difficulty is relevance. Youth of this century, with accelerated changes, and narrow focus, can't and don't relate to the links of the past. Here is where I question my relevance. Only because the experiences of my long life journey, applied in a historical context, were significantly influenced by monumental events. Monumental to me. Here's the rub, and I'm sure it's common to all, those events which marked my time so profoundly, are meaningless to most of today's youth. Where does that leave me? I try to keep pace. But as my role in life's drama continues to diminish, and I'm relegated to staring and comparing, I continue to redefine my relevance in time. I'm not complaining mind you, I'm just feeling self-conscious about the obvious changes to grapple with while growing older. So 2020 comes into view not so much with my touchstones, but with those of my offspring. I'm grateful.

Happy New Year!

10/29/19

I'm sure I have something to say, why else would I be sitting here typing. My problem is justifying writing at all. I look in the night sky and can't help being overwhelmed by infinity and the relation to the utter smallness of my thoughts. My time, our time, this time, passes so rapidly, sometimes I don't see the point in expressing thoughts, worthy thoughts, thoughts of past experiences, or even thinking at all. There's a futility in trying to find meaning. I find more meaning in futility. But then the human aspect emerges. We have to live together. So we better find some meaning in our common condition. You would think that would be a simple matter, like caring and sharing. Life is more complicated and there are so many factors in the human condition. Here is where I diverge because I get weighed down trying to balance our innate goodness with our obvious evil. Personally I find the scales tilted in favor of evil, visible in our constant greed, oppression and utter corruption. What then?

I turn to the children, specifically my grandkids. When the definition of love gets muddled on life's journey, for me it's rekindled in the moon light in their eyes, the sunshine in their smiles, the spring in their step, the gladness in their understanding, the realness of their hug. Their souls are free, but for how long? Right now I just wallow in their innocence and joy. When I'm with the little ones I'm transported, and thankfully so. At my age, remembering is a challenge, their antics, their laughter, their questions, all jog my memory. I can relive similar experiences, and smile in wonder at the human condition before...

Bless the children!

Where to begin? Why begin? What's to be said? I don't know. I just thought since it's been a couple months since I've blogged, sounds like clogged, well something needed to be written. The Labor Day weekend approaches and the holiday spirit collectively builds in the minds of the populace. As I remember the school year didn't begin until after Labor Day, which indicated the end of Summer. But now the kids are already back in the rigmarole of school days. Of course I'm not affected in any way shape or form. I'm an old man and can barely remember youthful times. My days whistle by with little variation and I don't mind. There's an ease to sameness which I now appreciate. Frankly most activities however inviting become an effort. I guess I'm referring to the upcoming holiday season. I really shouldn't go on about my self induced anxiety concerning the prolonged effort from now until the new year. So I won't. But just let me state if I had my druthers, I'd be a solitary curmudgeon.

So what else is new? My brother Casey stopped over the other day, and we had a very comfortable few hours catching up with family matters and sharing annoyances. We delved into our shared history and how our parents' divorce affected and changed each of us. We speculated on all the what ifs. Mostly we laughed at even the most traumatic of events, what else could we do? But in old age and having to continue the struggle, the good fight, well sometimes we wish we would have had some money, a formal education, mentors to guide us, aspects which would have helped us navigate the congested and murky waters of life. Regrets sure. We always return to our goof fortune, I mean good fortune. Sometimes we have to search for it. Then we laugh and that's where it starts. Humor is our foundation and what a foundation it is. It is the thread connecting the generations through hard times and celebratory times. My granddaughter tries to make me laugh, and she does to the extreme joy of us both. How much money or education do I need for such a sheer feeling of ecstasy.

Thinking of my granddaughter and the juxtaposition with my sister, her great Aunt, is disconcerting. My sister who knows the healing balm of laughter, also knows the heavy burden of loneliness, of extreme poverty, the despair of no hope, yet she forges on. She has more than tread the fierce rip tides of life, and did it alone. She's old and deserves a respite from all forms of burden. Sadness and struggle unfortunately are human's common legacy. Ain't that funny!

T oday is Saturday June 22nd, so it is officially summer. Frankly it doesn't mean a twit to me, because at my advanced age every day is the same, with little exception. Although the daylight varies so there's that. When I become aware of all that is happening around me, and be sure plenty is going on, street festivals, music events, art shows, etc. etc., I'm quite mentally motivated. But after further thought, like transportation, congestion, time restraints, distance, large crowds, noise pollution, jostling, lines, sunscreen, well you get the gist. I stay home. I visualize. I've heard it and done it all before anyway, so what's the point. I know, bad attitude. But that's my nature, if it don't come easy forget it.

I did have a wonderful experience on Father's Day. After some gentle coercion by my son, mainly having tickets, provided by his wife, the wonderful Doctor Lauren, Cassidy provided transport, I didn't have to get up early, we were off to the US Open Golf Championship. The event was held at the Pebble Beach Resort on the Monterey Peninsula near Carmel by the Sea. God's country. Or more like the rich people's country. It certainly was a once in a lifetime chance and I thank Cass and Lauren for that. I must say being on the world-famous golf links watching the greatest players in the game had moments of surrealism. The skies were grey and overcast with a marine layer. The temperature cool. The crowds were massive and enthusiastic. We surveyed the best viewing opportunities and got lucky with some but others were filled to the max. Along the 8th fairway we secured an ideal spot. A huge ravine, cliffs sloping down to the sea, dissected the fairway. The players second shot had to carry the chasm. A sliver of land was the only walkway to the green and we were perched right there. This vantage allowed all the players to walk past us no more than arm's length away. We could give them thumbs up, and shout encouragement as they strode past. Certainly a highlight of our experience and we have video and photos for proof. I play golf. Cassidy plays golf. I'm a fan and have followed the game since I was a boy. I know the history. My favorite players go back as far as the era of Sam Snead and Ben Hogan. The game has changed considerably but you still have to get the ball in the hole. So comparisons of different eras, different players, different equipment are fun to argue, the action remains the same. I was in awe of the course itself, set up to be a true championship test. I was in awe of the players and their mastery, their skill at conquering such a test. Or not. I was fortunate to share such a rare experience with my son, who knows my history with my dad and my uncle, himself a great golfer, who can appreciate the linkage of time to family through golf. I'm sure he'll endeavor to keep it alive with his family. We rode home in silence, it was late after all, but sometimes silence tells it all.

Love wins again!

06/02/19

Today is June 2nd, 2019. My brother Steve's birthday. And tomorrow is my sister's birthday. Susan will be 69 and Steve would have been 68. Unfortunately he died at 21. Sad. So today he's been dead 47 years.

My brother Steve. Frankly I barely knew him. I was three years older. Our young worlds really didn't overlap. And once our family disintegrated the separation between individuals became more obvious. He was a good boy and funny with a mischievous streak. I remember when he was very young he had asthma. My mom would set up a steam tent over his bed so he could sleep easily. He grew out of it though. One Christmas I won't forget. The family still pretended to be intact. Toys were scattered about in the living room and under the tree. We four kids were playing with new stuff and lounging in our pajamas. Steve was looking around and assessing and comparing Santa's gifts. When out of the blue he yells, "this is the worst Christmas ever!" I guess he didn't get what he ordered and my mom was chagrined. As we got older and our childhood became adolescence and teen, things really changed. I had become relatively delinquent and with my dad out of the picture Steve somewhat followed suit. He experimented with nonconforming styles, like Beatle boots and longer hair. He started to get in trouble. My mom, poor thing, was a basket case. She had no coping mechanism for out of control teens. Somehow she decided, and I'll never know how and who with, to allow Sue and Steve to become wards of the state. Both were shipped off to the state reform schools for boys and girls. So much for the post World War II, 1950's American family, it was over and radically altered forever. A shame. Steve survived his stint and actually thrived. He came home to finish high school. He developed a group of great friends and even was a star on the swimming team as the lead diver. So today I think of him and a time long ago, fading from memory more each day. Memory is all we really have and when that's gone, well it's time to go.

05/14/19

Since 2009 we have gathered as a family in Palm Desert for the Hanucup Golf tourney. Initially it was played in December and coincided with Hanukkah. Weather mandated a seasonal change and now it falls on Mother's Day weekend in the Spring. The name remains even though it's closer to Passover. Children play in the pool, sumptuous food is served constantly and we have our Friday morning tourney. Eight players teed up this year, all of varying degrees of competence, hence we use the handicap system to equal the playing field. Our winner this year was Adam Gautier, with a 31 handicap, edging out myself with an 11 handicap. It was great fun. Cassidy created these humorous introductions, and I wanted to save them.

Golf Introductions

From Cedar Rapids, Iowa, this golfer is the owner of 2 green jackets. As well as 2 gray sweatshirts and 3 white pullovers. A man who's social media presence rivals that of the Kardashians. A golfer who moves through life at the pace of a lawn bowling match. 3 time Hanucup champion: Tom Raher!

This next golfer's swing hasn't changed in two years, which was also his last swing. A man who needs no introduction. The dark horse of this tournament, and within his family. The king of cuisine. Captain of cutting. Chairman of chopping. The barista of the boardroom. Danny Brooks!

Next on the tee, an estate planner from Agoura Hills, CA. He's the lost member of the rat pack. And the proud owner of a back pack. A seasoned traveler who hasn't seen his own home since the last Hanucup, he plans on beating all of today's opponents.... with jokes and sarcasm. Let's hear it for Adam Gauthier!

Next on the tee, a fashion icon in his own mind; a golfer who's had more hairstyles than Lady Gaga; a man who keeps the local dispensaries in business. San Diego native and Former hanucup champion; Steven Dratler!

Next on the tee, a lawyer from Alameda, CA. This golfer is just excited he's getting fresh air. A former member of the Avengers, which is the name of his litigation team, he swings his driver like he's just mainlined a triple shot of espresso. Last year's runner up, Casey Kaufman!

First on the tee, the defending champion and family videographer; this guy has lanes reserved at Fantasy Bowling this evening at 11 if anyone wants to join, always representing the Bay and looking to be the first repeat winner, 1 time Hanucup champion, Cassidy Raher!

Next on the tee, from Rancho Santa Fe, Ca, this golfer returns to the Hanucup after a 4 year absence. After only playing his home course since then, he's most looking forward to getting back there as soon as possible. Ready to compete for the crown, Howard Dratler!

04/29/19

I was asked by a 17-year-old high school student studying in Switzerland, how old was I, what was I doing, what was my opinion of, and what was the mood and climate in society, especially the protests, of 1968. We've never met but I was happy to oblige.

My Response

Hi Natalie,

I'll try to be forthright and share a bit of my historical landscape. In 1968 I was 20 years old, and it really does seem like a very long time ago. I was serving in Uncle Sam's Army, having been drafted in 1967, and was stationed in Germany. Consequently I was isolated from actively protesting and the military mandates as little outside news, especially public outcries against the military, as possible. Let me go back a bit. Prior to service, as a teenager, and product of divorced parents and a radically dysfunctional family, I rebelled. I had black friends and lived with a black woman, while immersing myself in the black culture. I learned a great deal. Back to the Army. While hanging out in the barracks with black buddies, listening to the soul of Motown, the news of Martin Luther King's assassination spread like wild fire. Of course I was dumbfounded and tried to express my shock to my friends. But the pot was simmering and rage was palpable. They asked me to leave because, obviously as a white man, I was a symbol of all their oppression.

So you can imagine an entire society torn, the fabric frayed. The political climate as I quickly learned, was divided along racial lines and those pro and con for the Viet Nam war. The manifestations of this climate, this hurricane, were many. Blacks said no more, expressed by the Black Panthers, students opposing the draft protested and took over college administration buildings. The police, well they just got more aggressive. But still being in the Army, I was insulated and only slowly becoming aware of the push and pull of the right and left, and black and white. I saw who was being shipped to Viet Nam, and it wasn't Joe College. Poor whites and an inordinate number of young blacks were fodder for the whims of the military industrial complex. My philosophy on many things was evolving and expanding.

The events of 1968 radicalized and numbed me, and my opinions solidified then, have varied little. My opinion of the power elite and their class war hasn't changed. In '68 I was of the opinion, with the emergence of left leaning politicians, and the ongoing civil rights movement, that a thread of social justice and fairness for all, would seep or creep back into our collective consciousness. King was murdered, Kennedy was murdered, I'm afraid that opinion was short lived. Skepticism and suspicion ruled.

The protests went on and would go on for years. Young men were burning draft cards. The nightly news, which we saw very little on the base, reported the number of deaths each day. Families were divided, those believing in stopping Communism, and those who saw the war as waste. My time as a soldier was winding down, and I was becoming ever more grateful I hadn't been sent to Viet Nam. I believed it was wrong, and I didn't want to die. I was siding with the protesters more and more. I was frustrated and saddened, and after the horrific assassinations, my only sliver of hope was a Humphrey victory at the riotous convention in Chicago. He lost and my hopes were dashed. I guess '68 was when I actually became cynical. Cynicism resides firmly in my psyche.

Nothing has changed actually, from then to now, and I suspect things could be considered worse now. At the time, protests, passing civil rights

laws, ending the war, ousting Nixon, we mistakenly felt we made a change.
But look at what's happening now. Right wing governments are xeno-
phobic and fostering hate. Trump is building a wall and trampling on civil
liberties. Brexit has divided England. And if worrying about the social
climate isn't enough, our actual climate is teetering on collapse. The
protests continue for all manner of human rights, and here the police
continue to kill unarmed blacks without repercussions. A football player,
Kaepernick, protests police brutality and there's protests in the form of
white backlash. Racism. Endless war. Corruption. It's been 50 years and...

Natalie, I hope I haven't been to off putting, but I really don't see the
world through rose colored glasses. Although your mom's photos have a
positive effect. Thanks for listening. Good luck with the project and your
future!!

A snapshot or two of me in the Army, circa 1968!

02/23/19

So What?

I've been thinking that it could be possible to use this essay format for writing blog entries. It shows the date and title and formats the writing in an₅₃ easy to read block. Christine, my beautiful wife just returned from a baseball game at USF, where the Dons won. She was so excited she ordered a Round Table pizza. Actually it's not much of an excuse because tradition has it, we always have pizza on Friday night. It is Friday isn't it? Well the street lights just went on so we have to call the kids in from playing in the street. Oh they are all grown and have their own kids, how wonderful!

Trump: State of the Union

When I listen to and watch Trump, two physical reactions take place. First, I shake my head from side to side continuously. Second, I chuckle in rhythm with my head shaking. Why? Because I'm agog! My political consciousness goes back to the Kennedy murder. I'm old. So my head shaking has spanned many and varied presidents. And I've chuckled at the lies and hypocrisy of pretty near all of them. Although, in my opinion, Nixon and Little Bush have run neck and neck as the most absurd. But, at least, all of the previous "leaders" consistently, at one moment or another, were actually presidential. Until now!

Let me state, I'm not an educated man, but I've read a book or two, which I think qualifies me to be a bit critical in my observations. I'm certainly not critiquing the whole talk as if I was a PBS pundit, but a couple of issues touch me. Also Trump's style, his bullying, is of particular interest.

I thought his hour and a half sing-song address touched very little on the actual state of our union. His tired generalities, platitudes with no substance, and slogans were disingenuous to a fault. Why in God's name did he feel the need to resurrect World War 2 veterans, and, what appeared to be, a very uncomfortable Holocaust survivor? From my back row seat, I thought this prolonged display, totally irrelevant and misguided. I actually felt sympathy for the old boys, having been so exploited. Of course they may have relished the attention, I don't know. But I do know there's no shame in Trump's game, and his self-praise is embarrassing.

I recently watched, again, a few early episodes of *Mad Men*, a show reminding me of my dad during that period, and the inevitable demise and dysfunction of our family, but I digress. I was struck by the real similarities between Don Draper and Don Trump. I saw in the TV depiction of an era and its male dominated culture, exactly what Trump symbolizes. His whole agenda is an AD campaign, filled with unverifiable facts, lies, serious manipulations, jingoisms, slogans and fear. His goal of course is to sell a product the consumer, the voter, us, doesn't need.

His sales pitch for "The Wall" is simply astonishing, manipulating our fear. Our Fear! The Trump train continues thundering down the rails. The noise forces us to take notice even though we try to stifle it, to muffle it, to silence it, but it's inescapable. The bombast, the lies, the manipulations are relentless.

Once again I refer to a film, life imitating art or vice-versa, *The Taking of Pelham 123*. The similarity to the Trump train is unmistakable. A psychopath and his gang hijack a subway train and chaos ensues. The crazed leader threatens to kill everyone on board unless the city pays a large ransom. Sound familiar? Thousands of government workers are held hostage, unless "The Don" receives ransom money for "The Wall!" The saga continues.

Frankly, I feel like a hostage. I've spent the last two years trying to avoid the Trump train. I haven't publicly expressed my sentiments because I'm from a generation that doesn't talk about politics or religion. I don't follow "The Don" on social media, which, by the way, is another presidential travesty, and I tune out news concerning his shenanigans. That said, these have been some of my thoughts, and now I retreat to the shadows.

01/18/19

I've often heard the line, "live life to the fullest." What exactly does that mean? Usually I notice said refrain, after someone experiences a near death occurrence. Cancer patients in remission, near fatal car accident victims are some common proponents of grasping more tightly to what they've been given. And when given a second chance, just what is it we become more aware of?

When I put myself in those shoes and think how could I live life to the fullest, my mind reels. My perception or concepts tend to see exaggerated efforts, huge and risky endeavors, and experiences beyond mundane, daily activities. Like climbing Mt. Everest, parachuting period, single handedly sailing across an ocean, or hiking North to South America, things I'm not going to do.

Are these grand efforts and all they entail really living life fuller? Say you slip on Everest ice and slide to your death, or the chute doesn't open and wham, or a raging storm sinks your boat and you drown, well your fans can sing, he lived life to the fullest. I don't know, I tend to approach the idea of a fuller life a bit differently. Say I know I'm going to die, which I do, we all are, and I've been given a relative time limit. I ask myself, how can I be happy, or happier? What makes me happy and is happy what I want, and is happy equal to fullest?

Let me just interject, knowing I'm going to die does not make me happy. I'm a septuagenarian and have given considerable thought to the subject of a full life. I'm also a pragmatist and understand clearly, happiness (fullest) is personal and subjective.

Happy 1, marked by joy
Happy 2, marked by good fortune
Happy 3, eagerly disposed to be of service
Happy 4, well expressed and to the point

So if I stir these ingredients into the stew of a full life, I honestly don't see traipsing up mountains as a goal. I can though, use the examples of two figures I admire, Gandhi and Mother Teresa, who climbed mountains and sailed oceans daily, humbly smiling, fortunate to be in service to their fellow man.

I think it's important to realize a full life is a personal domain. The defining qualities of a full life are not determined by others, but by you. Various monks, Buddhists, Trappists et al, dedicate their lives to austerity, compassion, and harmony, attributes I consider quite fulfilling. This is where I turn inward on my quest for a full life. Knowing I don't have the resources or desire to triumph over obstacles like mountains and oceans, I can strive to see clearly – to see what makes me happy, calm and joyful and express it. Understanding is triumph. When I'm silent like now, thinking of these words and what they mean to me and trying to convey them, I'm joyful, I'm happy. Can't this moment be considered living life to the fullest? I say yes.

The funny thing is I apply this logic, my logic, to all my actions and observations. Each morning when a flock of geese honk their way over my house I revel in our connectedness. When the neighborhood children stop to play in my wife's fairy garden, and hold the small seashells to their ears, listening for the sound of the ocean, I appreciate the harmony. I can climb two city blocks and see both the Pacific Ocean to the West and turning East, the City's striking skyline downtown. My Everest. Most significant of this inward looking triumph is family. Logically I reflect, contemplate and dwell on my good fortune, which is my wife, my sons, their wives, and my grandchildren. This family web of consciousness spreads and covers most all my world. All that I see or do has links to family. Fullness.

I won't bore you with my medical history, but I can attest to being faced with the notion, "I better live my life to the fullest." What is the fullest? I subscribe to the idea, the mundane, our daily life, what we do and don't do, are the components necessary. Being aware, being aware of yourself and your surroundings. When you are sitting in your chair and worried about living your life to the fullest, you are. Know it.

P.S. I would be remiss if I didn't include a note about the flip side of living a full life. I have some experience in the field and I know more than a few who would discard or discount my earlier thoughts. Those, who would embrace the vices as a means to fulfillment, and shirk all responsibility while diving head long into final debauchery. Oh well, death awaits either way!

Doing nothing.

Doing nothing is nearly oxymoronic, because it implies the absence of action. Here in lies the conundrum. There is a great deal of activity, mostly mental, involved in doing nothing. Don't you love the sound of doing nothing, quite melodious. Actually that statement is the first of many thoughtful diversions in the art of doing nothing. Just imagine the time spent comfortably applying musical references, sounds, songs, rhymes, even visualizing dance routines, to the fluid, "ing" "ing" of doing nothing. I think you're getting the gist, or at least this simple example may set the tone for my explanation.

I've had just cause to try however ineptly to define doing nothing. The notion began harmlessly after I retired from regular, daily employment. Friends, relatives, acquaintances and strangers on the street, would ask, somewhat bewildered, what do you do now. What do I do now? Well my first reaction, being of a slightly confrontational nature, was to reply, whatever I damn well please, thank you very much! But I realized those good folks asking were generally curious, as most were of my age, and retirement loomed near and they were confused. I'd observed over time, work colleagues, as well as the average Joe, whether a bank executive or a lineman for the county, all stigmatized themselves, who they were, with the work they did. Their self-induced identity was job related, and hence their consciousness was burdened, chained unrealistically.

I first and foremost realized separation from the mental identity, the working you, was crucial in the transition to a new and better you, where anxiety plays a lesser role. But I found people's habits aren't easily changed or discarded. All I can say at this juncture is the more nothing you do, the easier it becomes. Doing nothing can take all day if you don't try too hard. There's another rather pertinent aspect to doing nothing, which ties into the work-related identity crisis, and that is guilt. Our Judeo-Christian culture is steeped in guilt. There's guilt for most everything we do, guilt for not coming to a complete stop, guilt for not saying I love you, guilt for calling in sick, guilt for ogling that beautiful woman, and the guilt goes on. Hence when you have nothing to do you feel guilty for not producing. But why?

I believe people wake up and think to themselves, if I don't do something my day is wasted. They feel guilty. Here's where I differ. In my long and happy journey to achieve nothing, or at least doing nothing, I've eliminated guilt. Some days it takes a good long while disassociating guilt with anything I'm not doing. Here we go, the art of doing nothing. My days are never wasted because what I do or don't do is guilt free. This concept allows a certain freedom – a freedom to open your mind and absorb. If you're letting the world in, through your silence, through your solitude, through your doing nothing, your senses are alive. The "ings" of living, seeing, listening, feeling, yes loving, these actions are the essence of doing nothing.

My point of course is doing nothing is full of action. The key then is learning, acknowledging, accepting the reality of the moment, then doing it, being it, enjoying it. When I make coffee in the morning I recognize it's only the beginning of my doing nothing. I have the good fortune, knock on wood, to live on a corner, with floor to ceiling windows. This particular environment is invaluable to doing nothing. I can spend an entire morning, and afternoon if I so choose, staring at a moveable feast, to use another author's fine line, out the window. Watching parents walking their children to school, staring at the regular dog walkers, and making sure their dogs don't poop on my stretch of sidewalk, checking out the senior ladies marching back and forth on their exercise walk, or and the most befuddling, watching the car parkers trying again and again to properly fit in a space too small. The thing about thinking is after a good long sample of all these endeavors, my mind searches the vault of memory for corresponding experiences. I can relive walking to school, the proverbial mile in the snow, I can remember the wild Weimaraner we had, who strew the neighbors' garbage all over the alley, I relive parallel parking with ease, to the astonishment of the officer monitoring the driving exam, all this and doing nothing. I say time well spent.

If thinking guilt free still seems less than adequate for doing nothing, there's the act of walking, which I consider doing nothing in motion. I will meander to the bank, well not really for there's no need anymore, to the deli, or to the post office. I always carry my iPhone that I admit is addicting. I especially use the camera to record and share interesting and unique visuals of our beautiful city. These meanderings can zig and zag leading me nowhere in particular, but when I return home I'm full of wonder – the wonder of doing nothing. And as the day wanes like the winter moon, I'm aware I haven't even read the next chapter of the more than a few novels I have at arm's length, or tuned into the intriguing detective series I love on cable tv. You see there is more of nothing I can save for tomorrow and the tomorrows after that. Doing nothing is time consuming and endless if you only embrace it.

I found as I age and my world shrinks, doing nothing can actually expand the world, the world that matters most to me, the world in my head, my mind.

Living

learn-ing

stand-ing

stare-ing

listen-ing

laugh-ing

sing-ing

touch-ing

love-ing

think-ing

walk-ing

feel-ing deeply

You get the picture, doing nothing is not doing nothing!

As Sam Wainwright said "See ya in the funny papers!"

I saw a photo posted on Facebook yesterday by a friend. She was at the super market and couldn't believe eggnog was already shelved in the refrigerator section. My anxiety level involuntarily spiked. The holiday season is truly upon us. It just means my tranquility, my solitude, my sugar levels are all being upset, altered, adjusted, compromised and I have to refocus.

Actually I had a preview of things to come the past two weeks. Fleet week roared into town, quite literally with the Blue Angels displaying their aerial delights. Also and at the same time, the Hardly Strictly Bluegrass festival rocked Golden Gate Park. I'm sure if you could view the city from high above it would appear overrun by ants. People everywhere! There were obvious obstacles to overcome, but each extravaganza was free and more than worthy. Excitement and enthusiasm was the general mood of all who came to share the wondrous entertainment. Multiple stages provided diverse musical talents and wandering from stage to stage, to hear your group of choice was the norm. The weather complied with the good attitudes, providing sparkling blue skies and comfortably warm temperatures. The clear skies was a blessing for the air show on the bay. Many years our normal fog pattern obscures any chance for the Blue Angels to perform their aerial acrobatics. Not this year, it was actually hot. For the extra million souls who descended on our fair city the weekend was satisfyingly spectacular. Since everyone was in such fine form and happy the inability to get anywhere without significant delays was a moot point. Thank goodness!

Following such an energy draining weekend, the next one was a combo plate. Remember at seventy going all day takes an inordinate amount of effort. But October marks special events in Raher history. My brother Casey's birthday begins the focus, albeit he handles activities from his end, and our involvement is nil. Our anniversary follows the next day. Then Ramsey's birthday concludes the three days of remembrance. Cassidy and Lauren treated us to dinner, celebrating our forty third wedding anniversary. We enjoyed casual and humorous conversation, which tends to be lacking in most family encounters, simply because the children demand so much attention. And rightly so. But it's always nice to ask questions and receive explanations without interruptions. I left pleased. Ramsey's simple birthday gathering was quite similar in the level of pleasure derived. Being with his son Rowan and basking in our blood linkage has a very life affirming element. Again the conversation over delicious pizza was easy, enlightening and needed. Lovely Reina educated me about ideas, I previously hadn't thought to delve into. For that I'm grateful. Of course being with family, sharing joy, absent of rancor, reinforces emotions and philosophies which guide our journey.

Although all of these events and encounters were rewarding, they were just a prelude to the onslaught yet to come. To clarify somewhat, all these heavy duty activities were semi spontaneous. Meaning they were sparked by a phone call, a time on a schedule or a notification. They weren't planned well in advance, so I couldn't dwell on the pros and cons, and incite my anxiety meter. Now the next couple months, populated with a string of holidays, raises the annual problems. Who, What, When, and Where. Yikes! Well maybe a cold eggnog will help!

07/30/18

Life expectancy, now there's a thought. I just turned 70 and what makes that number significantly different from other ages marked by birthdays, is the national average of the male's life expectancy doesn't extend beyond the 70's. Sobering indeed. Meaning what exactly, well, I won't see my grandchildren graduate high school, or marry. But that's alright. My three sons have accomplished enough to accentuate my existence with meaning and for that I'm at peace. One goal I'm striving to achieve is fifty years of marriage, and that is a joint effort, which pushes the boundary of that life expectancy number. You never know!

I spend time now remembering, comparing experiences, placing significance, and analyzing, applying regret or not, wondering how things might have been different, and do I really care. Second guessing is futile. Then there's perspective, how I view my life from this vantage point, looking back. I cringe at some of my youthful indiscretions. At the time they didn't seem significant, just thoughtless acts of expression, usually misguided. Experiences I hope to share by writing a small memoir, but I hesitate because time dilutes our ego driven self importance, and in the end my life like most all of us, is irrelevant in the grand cosmic chaos.

But getting old has its trials. First it doesn't help to spend much time looking in the mirror, because the person you see and the person you thought you knew can be radically different. The process of aging is so slow, well it does seem to accelerate the older I get, but the ideals, the ethics, the etiquette, the foundation for a persona, were built long ago. As I age and my perspective and tolerances change the foundation remains pretty much intact. Therefore when I'm bombarded by changes from the youth culture, I naturally resist for a time, until I compare my past to their present, and realize it's just the cycle of life. Perspective. Go with the flow, or drown!

The physical aspect of getting old is probably the most difficult aspect to reckon with. Activity use to be a defining characteristic, and to accept the erosion of that definition can be depressing. Playing, working, being extremely mobile become more difficult, even painful. Adapting without prejudice or bitterness, are key to remaining optimistic and hopeful, when all you really want to do is fall down a well of cynicism. Balance. Physical balance and mental balance, daily exercises which provide needed awareness. Walking and reading help.

I'm 70, I like to be quiet, and yell. I like to laugh, and cry. I like to listen to my heart strings, and watch the world go by. My grandkids remind me the children are worthy!

I've been in a slump. A reading slump to be exact. Once I read every day, but my habits have changed due in part to a cultural shift. At my age, old, I viewed technology, especially social media, inundate society like a tsunami. I lamented the loss of my comfort zone. What to do? I decided to embrace the change and the speed it was happening. My sons aided my immersion into the world of devices. I remember a time, which seems surreal, when a transistor radio was the only device necessary. The fear and trepidation facing me, while learning and navigating constant obstacles, took a while to overcome. I encountered a random voice with a certain explanation, which helped immeasurably. I learned intuition was the key. Intuition: instinctive knowing (without the use of rational processes). Here lies the poetic nature of interacting more comfortably in the digital world. Now when I get stuck, I don't cry for help. Usually no one is there anyway. I resort to intuition. I click icons backward and forward until the desired result is achieved. Risk and reward. The affect is tangible. Spontaneous, abstract, a degree of stream of consciousness are components I find in both poetry and the digital world. Surprisingly the time I once spent reading novels of choice, I'm now reading all sorts of random writing on line. I've adjusted. I think I read as much, but the source, the authorship, comes in waves and of varied lengths. Writing can be as short as a significant comment on a Facebook post, or as long as a featured article in the Atlantic Monthly. My effort is sporadic and the impact seems less. Albeit I've become more comfortable scrolling and navigating a tremendous range of sources, there is still a disconnect. Hence my slump.

So I take time to read novels, this is my current choice. Life is learning lessons. When you want to maintain a certain weight you push away from the table, or you stay out of the refrigerator. If you want to remain debt free you budget your money wisely. If you want to read and write you must portion your time accordingly. Easier said than done, right?

You know I consider myself a humble working man. I attempt to keep ego from most conscious acts. But there is a vein of vanity undeniably running through my mind. I've tried to instill small but poignant characteristics in my sons. Things like humor, simplicity, commit, loyalty, don't depend on others, work, be still, basic notions centering one's being. My vanity desires me to be remembered, in the grand cosmic scheme this is futile. In just a couple generations no one will know or care if I ever took a breath. Still I try. Even this blog is a meager attempt to leave a footprint in the sand.

Now grandchildren have populated my mental landscape and the reality of remembrance tugs stronger. So I'll share an example of my futility. I've commissioned a beautiful and significant painting for my son and daughter-in-law's new home. Auspiciously it's a house warming gift. But more than that, when my granddaughters look at it hopefully they will think of me. Here's where my fantasy expands. When my son gets old and leaves this painting to one of his daughters, and she has children, she can share the history of its meaning. My family has moved ever farther from the inner city and one day their progeny won't have an inkling of what urban life was like. But a cable car in a cityscape will or can be a starting point for tales of the past. My past!

11/08/17

Winter darkness has descended. I never like adjusting to shorter days. My rhythm gets confused. Daily rituals, if you can categorize them as such, because they do vary, manifest themselves at the wrong time of day. It's disconcerting. These small, mostly inconsequential variations, are just the tip of the proverbial iceberg. The avalanche of commercialism has begun. The "season" has emerged in full force. The abundance of candy (sugar) from Halloween has yet to be completely consumed, and Christmas bargains already inundate us. I'll admit my abhorrence for excess is a personal problem, the rest of the family finds laughable. I think I'm considered a lovable curmudgeon and do get infected with their holiday enthusiasm, albeit reluctantly. To enhance the commentary I'll add a couple of photos from the Halloween extravaganza.

So here you have me with the grim reaper. Don't we look like fast pals, it won't be long now! And the rest of the Rahers all decked out for "trick or treating" which was a smashing success. You see this is how these holidays play out. I see the negative side and resist with limited vigor, feeling it's hoopla over nothing. It's intrusive, it's obligatory, it takes effort, then the guilt for resisting, participation, and ultimately a fine time, simply a roller coaster ride of self induced emotions. Am I nuts? That's what I ask myself each morning over coffee. This was just Halloween, the heavy hitters are waiting in the wings. Thanksgiving, Hanukkah, Christmas, New Year, and throw in a birthday or two, and Veterans Day, well you get the picture. Sometimes I feel like a salmon swimming upstream. I love my family as individuals and I love being with them individually. But from a stress standpoint this is not my favorite time of year, but I'm sure when surrounded by smiling faces and the love that goes with them, I'll succumb to heartwarming joy. Lest they forget though, I'll remind them with my t-shirt!

08/04/17

T his past weekend I celebrated my 69th birthday. The significance of this particular one was the convergence of family. You see Brendan's family, which now included Quinn Rose (3 months) was coming from their home in Portland. This fact, meaning all of my sons and their offspring would be in one location at the same time, unusual, prompted me to invite my sister. We haven't seen each other in nearly a decade, and she has never seen her great grand nieces and nephews, so a perfect storm had emerged. After some logistical finagling all was set. She arrived. Brendan arrived. Brother Casey lives near so no problem there. Cassidy and Lauren opened their home for the festivities.

69 years old, wow! My memory swirls like I'm in a time tornado, visualizing myself as a youngster sitting at my grandfather's knee, looking up at his white hair, cigar smoke spiraling toward the ceiling, and thinking how incomprehensible and different older people and old age was. Bam! Now I'm my grandfather. How did I get here? Do my grandkids look at me and wonder, wonder if I ever played games, or ran fast, or laughed out loud, probably. I look at myself and wonder where it all went. The mind in all its trickery, desire, tells me, yes I can, but the body, the bones, the muscles, the physical screams differently. The swirling continues as my life and all the phases, phases I've nurtured and wish lasted forever, phases leading to destruction, halted abruptly and dismissed, phases I return to periodically to remember, all swirling in the tornado of my mind. Yet here I stand. Fortunate! I've learned a few things, while trying to stay awake during this lifetime. It's pretty simple really, and fundamental, don't dwell on the past so that it paralyses you, and don't be anxious about the future so it paralyses you too. Well, that leaves trying with some effort to live in the

present. I guess at 69 it's a bit easier to live in the present, because the future is at arm's length and the past, you know what they say, the memory is the first to go.

So having my siblings with me, who knows when that will happen again, if ever, meant a great deal.

I also think the significance of our convergence worked in reverse. My sons and their wives and children have never seen the Raher crew together, so I'm sure they all derived some insight into the strengths and flaws DNA hands down to those unsuspecting progeny. Never the less they are Rahers and will carry that name come what may. I might add, now in the present, having family, a family that not only survived but will now thrive, fills me with immeasurable joy, pride, satisfaction and tears!!

E veryday I think of my past, what I can remember. Age, getting old, is by far the impetus for such incessant remembering. The journey from one time, youth, to another time, now, is littered with sign posts. Some were heeded, others obviously not. Now, retrospectively, I can analyze choices made, and the ramifications which occurred. Which brings me to regret. I have to admit, I have many regrets, but what, if any, role do they play in my everyday life. No role whatsoever I say. Sitting here, at this computer, writing what I think, is a blessing. A blessing, because I made a wrong choice, or many wrong choices, long ago? Maybe, a decision which in turn led me to these words. So should I regret that, as a wrong turn somewhere in the past. No. Value is defined in one sense, the quality (positive or negative) that renders something desirable or valuable. Now able to express myself, is most desirable, therefore has a great deal of value for me. Hence the journey of life, following or avoiding sign posts, zigging and zagging whimsically, or despairingly, is defined by the desire of that moment. All valuable in the end.

It's the Christmas season. When I think of seasons, I think of Nature's seasons, or a baseball season, in other words a lengthy period of time. The Christmas season has become, or maybe it always was, much too long. But what is intrinsically desirable (valuable) about Christmas is the convergence of family and friends. I like Christmas movies. Movies that depict grown children returning to their family homes. The notion of wallowing in familiar sights and aromas. Seeing a bedroom untouched by time, or a dad snug in a worn chair watching football, a mom stirring a holiday tradition in a large bowl, siblings arriving with presents and smiles, is what we anticipate and desire. The value of the season.

Sentimental. I'm sentimental for memories and experiences in the future. A regret, of course. I'd love to witness my grandchildren returning to their childhood homes as adults. When I visit my son's homes, I see the incubation, the embryonic stages of holiday traditions. It warms my heart, simply because they are extensions of our traditions, desires, values and they will nurture and augment them for posterity. As I slip and slide off this mortal coil, I'm blessed with family, sentiment, regrets, all extremely valuable. I guess I'm valuable!

06/29/16

I noticed a hardness in my midsection. I didn't worry because I assumed it would go away. A few weeks passed and the condition seemed slightly worse. I decided to go to the doctor. It had been awhile since my last physical, so my visit would provide a proper overview. After I explained my concern, my doctor conducted his brief examination. To my surprise, he asked if I'd experienced intravenous drug use. I said yes, some 35 years earlier, why? My liver was enlarged and blood work was immediately ordered. Boom! I had Hepatitis C and some cirrhosis.

Shock! How could this be? I knew but still couldn't believe it. My mind reeled. There wasn't a cure. My liver would deteriorate until it no longer functioned, and I would die. This thought wracked my mind. I was tormented by the notion of my youthful indiscretions, stupidity and arrogance. The anger and futility of not knowing until it was too late, haunted me. Why would a virus wait 35 years to raise its ugly head. Certainly this was a cruel and unusual punishment for such a minor infraction.

Hmmm...resilience, courage, sense of humor! Good judgement comes from experience...experience comes from bad judgement.

I look in the mirror. I shudder to think a disease is working overtime to kill me. I look so normal and vibrant. I feel cheated, cheated out of a good portion of my life. I didn't do anything wrong. I feel like I'm on death row, for a crime I didn't commit. Worry!

Time passes. More tests. Explanations about treatment. Wait!

How will it come this death? I only hope suddenly and unexpected. But I dare say that probably won't be the case. Yet, I don't want to linger, feeble, with staring eyes reminding me of what I'll miss. Dying is fearful, but paradoxically has a calming effect. Simply put, all my other incidental manias and anxieties have been relegated trivial.

Never discount prayer. I invoke the Prayer of St. Francis: grant that I may not so much seek to be loved, as to love. For it is in giving, that I receive, and it is in dying, that I'm born to eternal life.

The night time is the worse. Sleep comes grudgingly. I think of the death process. The blood flow dammed in the liver, nutrients never reaching their destination. Toxins build and spread, I turn yellow. Sleep!

Daily life goes on. Family obligations and social functions, all provide necessary distractions from my self-examination. Never the less it continues. I think of the books I haven't read, and the ideas I haven't said. All the unseen components which are me, and I'm saddened.

Now begins the treatment. Interferon and Ribavirin. Pills and injections, constantly for a full year, with a success rate of maybe 30%. Needless to say the side effects were significant. The earlier mental anguish, was replaced or expanded by pharmaceutical induced depression, fatigue, nausea, anemia and all manner of grumpiness. Denying depression and moodiness, when questioned by loving family members, became difficult. Trying to act normal or enthusiastic about others, when I didn't want to be bothered, was a concern. At any rate, everyone weathered the storm, including me. Unfortunately, the first blood test after completion of treatment showed high levels of the virus. So it was all for nought.

I was glad it was over. My attitude changed. I figured the slow pace of the virus would still allow me a relatively long life. I rid my psyche of negativity, and focused on all that's positive. Grandkids. Exercise. Sons. Dear Wife. Extended Family. Nature. Goodness. Mindfulness. Humor. and the list goes on! I decided to get on with it, and I did. Although, I did keep abreast of what was happening with Hep C trials. I knew companies were close, and FDA approval was all that was necessary for new drugs. I lived my life like nothing was the matter. Lo and behold, as 2014 drew to a close, Harvoni came on the market. It was exciting because the treatment was only three months, one pill a day. The success rate was nearly 100%. I believe I was one of the early recipients. I was skeptical of course. But three months after completion, the benchmark, the virus was gone, kaput, undetectable, cured!

I was sixty years old when this roller coaster ride began. My wife and I raised three sons and they have given me four grandchildren. I worked all my life. Reminiscing about the random chaos of the late sixties and early seventies, and how I successfully survived, gives me peace of mind. Now at sixty-eight, another bout won, I'm pleased to witness my progeny, and proclaim, Hallelujah!

For some reason my attention span, my due diligence, my ability to concentrate, have been under attack. My will power has mysteriously abandoned me. I've done some soul searching, and analyzing daily habits or lack of, and have come to the conclusion, social media and it's addicting capacity, is the very culprit. I've been spending unnecessary amounts of time wandering in cyber space. For what? Not very much indeed. A lot of trivia, some useful, most not. An overwhelming amount of depressing politics, and entertainment news that I can't even relate to. I need to step back, push away, set down the iPhone, and go to the book store for long delayed purchases, and write, here.

50 years! A long time right? I look around and one social phenomenon trending for quite awhile now, is tattoo art, or ink. The reason I've pondered ink, is I've witnessed the evolution, or devolution, of this form of personal statement. Which I find, certainly from a distance, indecipherable, but sometimes attractive. Why would I care, well I have a tattoo. It is a daily reminder of a time etched in my memory. A time of rebellion, a time of stress, a time of upheaval, a time of aloneness, experiencing the rawness of life. A time of actions without regard for consequences, and there were many. One such reckless act was drinking beer as a teenager, in a car full of buddies, riding around at night, trying hopelessly to impress each other. Well it seems we were impressing a police cruiser, who happened to be following us. As we turned a corner, the only recourse was to hurl a six pack of beer out the window. Needless to say that ploy didn't save us from detection, as the cops saw what happened, and immediately flashed their lights, and hit the siren, pulling us over. Busted! Well this was the first step in getting a tattoo.

Naturally I was arrested, detained and charged with possession of alcohol as a minor. I was 17, a senior in high school, but had, I thought undeservedly, in the eyes and attitudes of the authority, a reputation as a juvenile delinquent. Needless to say I was made an example, to deter other potential delinquents, and received the rather harsh sentence, of 90 days in the county jail. One education was ending and another was beginning. The finality of a jail cell door clanging shut, requires an immediate mental adjustment. At 17 I learned stoicism and silence were tools needed to guard against chaos. I settled in and watched. After some time, a gregarious character approached and asked if I wanted a tattoo. I was aware, jail and the military were the only places tattoos were accepted and encouraged. I asked questions about the method, and he told me it was simple enough. Wrap a wad of thread around the point of needle, and dip it in a small bottle of India ink. He would then dab the needle point into my arm repeatedly. Time consuming for sure, but we had plenty of that.

What should it be? I didn't know, but common in jail houses were the usual: mom, a girl friend's name, born to lose, different numbers, hearts, assorted simplistic ink, vacant of any intellectual depth. Since I was at rock bottom and didn't give damn, I chose born to lose. And since marijuana or refer madness, was associated with outcasts and delinquents, the number 13 was added. You see M is the 13th letter of the alphabet. Jail house mentality at its finest. So I sat there day after day, while he poked at my arm. I felt I was sitting for a portrait. Only my tattoo would last longer. Do I regret it, sure, it's one of many regrets. When I shuffle off this mortal coil, who really cares. On the balance sheet of life I've gained far more than I ever lost.

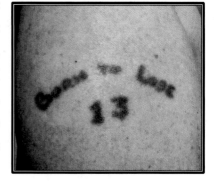

I just spent a truly wonderful and important weekend. Christine and I celebrated our 40th Wedding Anniversary. She orchestrated the entire weekend like a maestro conducting an orchestra. My three sons and their families honored us with their presence, their humor, support, and doing all that was asked, without hesitation. A grand dinner was shared, with applicable toasts, and a poignant poetic reading by all three men. Quite moving indeed. The children must have sensed the familial aspect, because they were all angels.

The next morning, Sunday, we attended 10:30 Mass. After Mass the families gathered again, to witness Father Koepland administer our marriage vows, again. It was a brilliant ceremony. The children encircled us on the altar, while we repeated the sacred vows. Many photos were taken, capturing our historic moment. We are extremely proud. The caravan returned to our humble abode, where Christine prepared a sumptuous buffet. A relaxed, banter filled afternoon ensued. Pictures were taken, babies hugged, puzzles arranged, baseball watched, the weary napped, and I basked in the glorious love! Amen.

The Rahers
By Brendan, Cassidy and Ramsey

On this, the day we celebrate your love,
Four decades you are matched like Giant gloves.
The Rahers gather to discern just how,
You managed to survive and thrive 'til now!

THOMAS RAHER

For on this special anniversary,
We watch Sir Thomas and his sweet Pee Wee.
While none of us were there when sparks did fly,
Our ode to them I'm sure will make you cry.

Because it tells the tale of what it means,
To be the offspring of such faded genes.
A story not without its ups and downs,
Yet laughter is the Raher's maiden sound.

And now, I turn it over to the one,
Who started all the raucous and the fun;
And changed your peaceful lives from two to three,
The eldest Raher son, his story please:

The year was nineteen seventy five
Two wandering hearts came alive
Within the beauty of our City
Two loves began a storied family

We stand here tall and full of pride.
You filled forty years with a wild ride.
You gave us names and life to live
I pass this love to your grandchild

So much to say, we're still together
A modest legacy to last forever.
Blessed was I with two younger brothers
Friends for life like no other.

Since the day I was born, laughter and love
Were given to me with kisses and hugs.
Dad taught me to throw, to ride my first bike,
I knew real early we were so much alike.

Once with my dad, laying atop his bed,
We waved, not our hands, but our toes instead.
A silly goof, so sarcastic at heart,
He taught me humor from the very start.

Mom made us costumes, thought outside the box,
Took care of us through itchy chicken pox.
She made us eat healthy. No Doritos.
I'll always love her famous burritos.

One Christmas Eve, we got to open some toys.
Dad got emotional watching his boys.
I looked up at him, and I asked him why.
"I'm just so happy," with a tear in his eye.

You're now grandparents of four little ones.
Remember a time you had just three sons?
Speaking of three, lil' Bren was your third,
He'll share his thoughts in his very own word.

To be the youngest brother of such gents,
You'd think I'd shrink and bow in discontent.
For battles of my strength I'd often fail.
But like my mom, my humor could prevail.

So watching her, I found just when to jest.
Her savvy wit could always pass the test.
A cunning skill that means the world to me,
A gift I pass with grace to Grant Tommy.

My dad, he taught me how to find the peace,
Of pie and mind, both rich with sweet release.
With chess, he showed me how to play it out
Be graceful in defeat and not to pout.

Both mom and dad ignite our inner light,
And grant us time and space to get it right.
We can admit without a hint of play,
Without their love, we'd never be this way.

Happy 40th Anniversary

08/10/15

"Before bed tonight, Ashby and I were chatting about living a long time, and how she'll be old like me when she has kids, and I'll be the 'papa' to her kids. Then she said, as she almost started crying, 'I hope papa and grandma kooky never die!'

My son related this poignant repartee to my wife and me, and we were truly moved. Ashby is a lovely and precocious child, and astonishes us with her grasp of complicated concepts. In all honesty, growing old is disconcerting to say the least. The balance between the mind and the physical body has tipped in the wrong direction. Once, I thought therefore I could do, but all has changed. Doing takes calculation, even after you THINK, no problem I can do that. The reality of deterioration, however daunting, always seems trivial and insignificant, when embraced by the unconditional love of the little ones. Their innocence and sharing is not prejudiced by age or gender, old people are just fine with them. My problems, drift away when I'm in their virtuous presence.

06/09/15

"Tommy I want u to know that you cut the trail and showed a lot of people the way, hope u know that. Special special spirit."

This is a quote from a friend from my youth. Mike Casey was diagnosed with lung cancer last year. It was a bitter pill to swallow for a fun loving kook like Mike. He battled valiantly but to no avail. He died earlier this year. He reached out to his many friends, subtlety, through Facebook messages, and old photo sharing. The lead quote he shared with me, and I was humbled and honored that, my misguided youth was somehow influential to those around me. Mike will be missed.

Dennis Turner: "Tom...really...the influence u have had on so many lives...it always felt like there were at least four of you...i always found u a little scary...but count me among those whom u have given ur love and a kind nudge towards home. u have that gift that grows as u give it away."

An old, and each year when I say old friend it becomes more literal, friend has flattered and humbled me with his expression. We go along trying our damnedest to stay out of our own way, and even more so, out of the way of others, especially family and friends. So when a remark like the one Dennis allowed glides pleasantly by, your heart sings a little louder!

05/22/14

Since I'm slightly obsessed with posting, sharing, publicizing, and linking my activities, here is another attempt. I received my first copy of my new book, and Christine recorded the opening ceremony. My excitement is never too ostentatious, and I was a bit tongue tied. But hey, that's what this blog is for, putting down any and all of my thoughts and, or actions.

A few things, (I love using the word thing, it expresses and defines all of what I want to say and can't find the word or words), stand out from the recent past. Some I can illuminate with photos and some I can't. I'll start with a phenomenon which has caused me much concern and anxiety. As my family and friends know, (and probably the only people who might actually read this), I have Hep C, which advances slowly yet inexorably. The new year has brought forth a rash of new and effective drugs, which all pharmaceutical companies are racing to get approved and market. Very costly I might add. I've reconnected with my doctor and done all the preliminary screening, and with my constant prodding, shall soon embark on another treatment. We are just waiting for the FDA to approve the drug I will combine with an already approved drug. What makes these new drugs better? Well the success rate is virtually 100%, the treatment length is 3 months, instead of 12, with no injections, oral only, and the side effects are less debilitating. So that's that!

Now, we were downtown running an art errand. After that interesting encounter concluded, we decided to walk around the corner to the John Spence Gallery and view the art on display. Most of the remarkable paintings were well out of my price range, except one. One of the last viewed struck my fancy and I immediately inquired about purchasing it. Ironically the person I asked, who was working the desk, happened to be the artist. He was pleasantly surprised and we had an explanatory chat. The young artist was a graduate of the Art Academy, like most of the artists whom I've collected. It was a perfect meld for both of us.

12/06/13

I wanted to acknowledge family members, and Mid-Westerners in general, a hearty lot indeed, after the devastation reeked recently, by a swarm of tornadoes, tearing through Washington Illinois, specifically. Luckily my Aunt Rose was spared the heart wrenching destruction, so many of her neighbors were not. I sometimes feel the relief agencies, i.e. government of all levels, the media, have a tendency to down play local, down home disasters, in direct contrast to other disasters around the globe. This life changing occurrence, certainly was short lived on the national consciousness, but I'm sure those affected didn't care. They don't sit around waiting for distant help, they get busy. They come together, a unified front, and everyone pitches in. They accept, without pity, their situation and figure the best remedy for all. Inclusion not exclusion. Children learn the finer qualities of the human spirit, watching their parents perform admirably. I appreciate this characteristic!

11/07/13

I was meandering through iPhoto, which I rather like doing, because we have thousands of photos, depicting family members and experiences. Many get passed over for being unremarkable. In any event they are stored on the computer. Periodically I'll wade in and delete as many irrelevant photos as I can manage. I do get waylaid more often than not by my mesmerizing granddaughter, Ashby. She shuns, for the most part, posing for pictures, although she acquiesces, when family pics are required. I'm always taken aback when I see her frozen in time, with expressions, or actions, suggesting an entire universe behind those absorbing eyes. She never fails to draw me in. I try to imagine what she is imagining. The wonder I see, is wonderful to me, and reminds me the film of callousness I've nurtured over a lifetime, is useless. Enjoy!

Mortality. Something you never think of in the throes of youth. But that's what we have birthdays for. When you're young and trying to make heads or tails of things, the future seems endless, and setbacks and possibilities are daily occurrences. If you're lucky, you'll find a tolerable job, or even better, do what you like and get paid for it. Maybe even find someone and create a family and a world. Again your consciousness is constantly in the now. Time. Age. One day the chaos, the duty, have all moved outward from your world, the world you created, the notions, the ideas your identity is built on. Well I shared this dilemma recently with my little brother, an old reference to a time when he was smaller than me. Both our families are grown. It was his 59th birthday. I'm 65. We sat talking over lunch, about being our grandparents' age, yet still seeing the world through youthful eyes. We realized the end was much nearer than we cared to admit, and the prospect of new journeys, were appropriately pipe dreams. Hope was finding contentment in no regrets. And we laughed. If there was one bonding ingredient in our relationship, it was the ability to laugh, loud and heartily at life and its paradoxes. We will forge on, flaws and misgivings, simply because people are depending on our laughs!

S ince I'm trying to catch up and make my blog current, here's more. I'm staring. Staring is part of my quest for calm, and my expansive view provided by floor to ceiling windows, helps immeasurably. The sun's lower, winter, trajectory creates long shadows. Long shadows, for me, trigger waves of nostalgia. Nostalgia for what? Certainly not a fractured youth, and all the missteps and wrong turns. But more a nostalgia for a sensibility, a vision, a day dream, a moment when you transcend the now, and soar. I was reminded recently of a transcendent sense which over-whelmed me some 40 years ago. I arrived in San Francisco, a self-appointed dharma bum, and stumbled into Vesuvio's. Needless to say it was a revelation. I immersed myself. Wallowing in the open dialogue of artists and poets, transformed me, and I had found my mental center, in this salon society. I had cause to revisit such a sensibility a couple of weeks ago, as Vesuvio's was celebrating 65 years as an institution of avantgarde' intellectualism. I no longer frequent, with regularity, this haven, that nurtured and fostered my evolving thought process, but being there for this anniversary stirred more than a few grand memories.

09/04/13

Fall is upon us, of course here in San Francisco, the seasons vary ever so subtlety. Also the time has been altered by an hour, which used to be a concern, but now it's just another bump in the road. It doesn't affect me one way or another. My pursuit of maximizing my solitude, and fortifying my calmness is hardly impacted by time. Let it flow. It is my intent though, to chronicle some of what happens in the course of that unceasing flow, and frankly the people and experiences in my life only work to embellish positively, my journey. These ideas, thoughts and observations, I'd like to highlight with some corroborating photos. So first, a few heart warmers of my granddaughter Reese. Like me she loves pasta, and I should also wear a bib when I eat it.

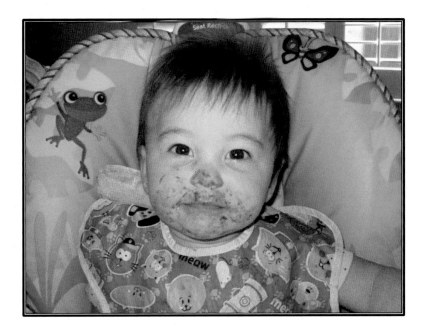

08/27/13

I keep thinking, and this goes on and on, about buying a tire pump for my bicycle, at the hardware store. But I don't. My alter ego seems to think I need to live longer, impress the multitude, and lose weight, or at least the midriff causing me anxiety. And riding a bike is supposed to be an ingredient, one of several, which will help. But here I sit in an ever deteriorating 65-year-old body, screaming why bother. Now a days exercise just induces nagging pain in my back, leg joints, lungs and leaves me depressed knowing I'm incapable of, what once came so easily. I'm considering joining the Y, so I can use the elliptical machine, the stationary bike, and treadmills, but that takes a mental commitment, which I know I would squander, and then feel guilty about the monthly fees. You see I've calculated most scenarios, and have for a long time, but now the reality of physical age has become a major factor. Too bad. Recovery time is longer, diet and nutrition are much stricter, just trying to stay in some kind of shape needs radical reform. But what am I willing to try, and do I even care. Today I went lawn bowling, which is hardly aerobic, even though motion is required. A rather high degree of skill is necessary to compete, and the social interaction is nothing but positive, so in the larger scheme of things, I consider this activity worthwhile. It certainly doesn't reduce my waistline, but it makes me feel good. What more can I ask.

04/19/13

I finally had a chance last week to take the bus downtown, specifically skid row. There is a vacant hotel standing idly on the corner of 6th and Howard. It has been designated for demolition for new development. The interesting thing is for the past 16 years it has been a work of art. A virtual sculpture. There are, miraculously, chairs, TV's, refrigerators, beds, sofas, lamps, any and all types of furniture protruding from the windows on each floor. I've driven by hundreds of times, always marveling. Here are a few photos depicting this unique and doomed work of art.

I was lawn bowling yesterday, on a warm San Francisco afternoon, and a friend asked when I was going to update my blog. I thought to myself, hmmm, good question. This blog site has taken a relative back seat to all the other activities out there, in social media land. I also get the sense that no one actually visits here, which minimizes my motivation to keep it current. But I suppose someday my children will resurrect these postings out of sheer curiosity.

It's been a long 4 months since I last visited this space and it has occurred to me, one very special event has changed my life, and all of our family's lives. Reese Casey Raher was born on December 8th, and for you Catholics, the feast of the Immaculate Conception. In her short 3 months, she has grown chubbier, now laughs at the least prodding, and so far has a wonderful disposition. We were graced the past two weekends, having the little ones, Reese and Ashby, stay with us. It's such a joy to witness the speed of their mental development. Ashby is really smart, and has an imagination that is far beyond her nearly 3 years. She'll sit in her little rocking chair, watching the cars go by, and exclaim how they are lions and tigers. I better add a couple pictures at this point.

It seems the photos automatically insert themselves where paragraph breaks are. I found a couple more I like. One I especially like because Ashby has captured my expression, which is peacefully watching golf on TV. I've titled it "Zen and the Art of Golf Viewing." Anyway the girls have naturally become major players in my life. People, places, activities, I once considered so significant in my life, have in some cases just disappeared. Do I miss them, well not really. At my age, I'm a completely different person. Although I remember what once moved me, and cling to some aspects, like the music, the ideals, but I don't have to preach, or sell what I think is right. I can just observe the little ones get smarter and smarter, and rejoice. Maybe I had a little something to do with the family river as it grows and spreads like a delta. When I look into their eyes, I feel good that I passed this way.

11/09/12

Recently my wonderful son, Cassidy, and his even more wonderful wife, Lauren, decided to generously treat Christine and myself to two nights in Carmel-by-the-Sea. We were luxuriously sequestered at the Carmel Country Inn B&B. The ambiance, the hospitality, the sumptuous buffets, were all superb. We strolled the narrow lanes taking in the sights, noticing the restaurants, the art galleries, the novelty shops, the chocolate arcade, and enjoying the relaxed atmosphere.

For me the highlight of the mini-vacation was playing Pebble Beach Golf Links. Through one of Cassidy's college buddies, we were able to secure a tee time, no easy feat. If that wasn't enough, we were blessed with absolutely perfect weather conditions. Another rarity on the Northern California Coast. Cassidy drove down from the Bay Area for the special occasion, and we shared a cart, as well as sharing this unique experience. Christine had her own cart and acted as the official film maker, enjoying her duties, as well as the natural wonderland. We completed our round as the sun set on Pebble Beach and we smiled all the way to the parking lot, basking in our delight. A special memory for sure!

S hades of Pink, the sartorial theme for Cassidy's 34th Birthday. Lovely Lauren reserved a mid-morning tee time at the renowned "The Bridges Golf Club." The sky was slightly overcast, allowing for moderate temperatures throughout. The course was in excellent condition and Brendan's constant wit had us in a jovial mood.

This wonderful photo highlights the joy we all shared, celebrating Cassidy's day. We were nearing the end of the round, which arrived all too soon. The grand club house in the background awaited. Cassidy and I always compete for bragging rights, and fortunately for me, on this auspicious occasion, I prevailed. Not by any brilliance on my part, but simply by the three double bogeys he closed with. Too bad son. Brendan showed signs of true golfing talent, and of course kept us in stitches with one non sequitur after another. A grand time indeed!

When we returned home, Lauren had the fixings for a scrumptious dinner. A chocolate cake was baking in the oven, and the youngsters (Cass and Bren) were lying about, trying with all their might, to keep their eyes open. This lovely photo depicts Ashby's fecund imagination, as she imitates her mom's efforts, in her own miniature kitchen. Such a wunderkind!

Well now, obviously the cake is out of the oven and cooled. Dr. Lauren spread a thin layer of frosting, and now Christine is applying the birthday decorations. Christine also known as, Grama Kooky, is barely able to get the icing on, before Ashby, our little Giants fan, can finger it off. They both look intent on accomplishing their tasks. Both are too adorable!

And in keeping with our Pink Theme, we were startled on our relaxing ride home, by this amazing rainbow. We were cruising down the freeway, discussing all the small joys we experienced during the wonderful day. As we were crossing the Bay Bridge and listening to the Giants game, Jon Miller was exclaiming on the radio, about the incredible rainbow. This natural wonder was a most fitting culmination to a day of many wonders. Family!

01/30/12

There seems to be a serious gap in blog postings. Why? I think it's the post-holiday blahs. All my natural rhythms, creatively speaking, were compromised. I'm sensing a resurgence of focus. This sensibility is manifested first physically, with a hint of exercising activity, and then with a clear mind tasks are completed. I'll admit our very temperate winter weather is a major factor in a timely recovery. There are very few things, like warm sunshine, for much needed motivation.

The holidays lasted over a month. It is indeed a test of endurance. Albeit each event was joyful and memorable. This positive characteristic is attributable to each and every family member, whose only goal was to share love. So I had little opportunity to express my cantankerousness.

My generous in-laws, Larry and Linda Brooks, invited everyone to their annual Hanukkah extravaganza. It's a fantastic food fest, surrounding the celebratory traditions. Larry has instituted a Hanukkup golf tournament, which is my highlight of the weekend. All the lads joyfully participate, but there is a slight undertow of serious competition. A traveling trophy (Hanukkup) is presented to the winner. It is a wonderful day of golf!

The conclusion of the long season was a lazy day at my house. After Christmas Mass, the local clan staggered over for Christine's non-traditional afternoon meal. We decided against another bite of turkey or ham. Instead we wallowed in the comfort of endless Sloppy Joes and chips. It worked for me!

There you have a partial and brief catch-up. Stay tuned.

10/28/11

W here have I been? Recently or presently, they are the same for the most part. I cling to now, but time stretches and bends, until remembering is difficult. So I'm circling, constantly circling, inside the confines of my cranium. My mind sails like a very slow rotating tornado, much of life's debris sticks, good and bad. While it's circling I gauge and select what's pleasing and store it. Of the debris that's less desirable, I allow it to spin out and back into the never ending flow of flotsam. Of course time re-asserts itself and the now, presently, becomes recently, and I have to start again, adjusting, selecting, detaching, waiting and wondering. These processes are continuous and sometimes I have to put my foot down and say no, no more. Distractions help, like a round of golf, or a game of lawn bowling, even a walk to the ice cream shop. Here I'm lucky, grateful, to be retired, because I can ponder while wandering and give new meaning to doing nothing. Yet circling. And when I share time with my granddaughter I realize the circle has encompassed her, and I know I'm blessed!

10/11/11

O n this day 36 years ago, Christine and I were wed. What can I say, where did the time go? It is difficult to wrap my mind around all that's transpired. So many memories, great and less than great, so many changes, changes that reminded me, sometimes shockingly, that complacency wouldn't work. I'd arrive at a comfort zone, and naively think, I got it, and it would last forever. Change and adjustment. This thrust and perry through life was labeled maturity, but I still can't put my finger on it. I think it can be defined a bit more glumly as old age. Only the changes continue, slightly more excruciating because of the added effort. But the rewards are truly graceful. Three sons, who keep me laughing and crying, and living as an emotional human. They have provided me with the concrete foundation to weather any and all oncoming storms. For this I'm ever so grateful. This journey Christine and I have been treading, one of resoluteness, has been tempered with love. A loving family, hey not so bad!!

10/03/11

Good morning. It's Monday. The sky is overcast and light showers are dampening the sidewalks and asphalt. That indescribable aroma of warm, moist concrete is wafting upwards. I think of it as the smell of humidity, if that's even possible. I'd like to briefly recap a couple of noteworthy experiences. Of course you probably know, the Bluegrass Music Fest was nearby in Golden Gate Park. Friday morning before the constant wave of humanity converged, the music was free after all, I walked over to hear an old crony. Charlie Musselwhite was opening the proceedings and his classic blues style is always a treat. We had been emailing in the past about Hepatitis C. We shared medical information, treatments, resources, and side effects, and what to expect and dealing with the slow moving disease. Charlie like most of our ilk sings and lives the blues.

Saturday was different. I was surprised by an unexpected musical performance. A preface; As a retired (euphemism for lazy) person I choose not to be serious or productive every waking hour. Consequently I've latched onto a couple of trivial melodramas on the evening TV schedule. *House* is one of them. Well I was delightfully stunned to find out Hugh Laurie is an accomplished musician. The night before I saw him live in the park, PBS had a *Great Performances* episode of he and his band playing in New Orleans. Inspiring indeed. But Saturday I was drawn out-of-doors, not only by Hugh, but some fine young family members, Lisa from LA, Isaiah, new to this world, and the effervescent Danny and Teresa. We wove our way into the throngs for a comfortable spot. The company was spot on, and Laurie played a set resembling quite closely his PBS special. A fine time.

Sunday my focus and energy shifted completely. It was time for serious golf. You ask, how can golf be serious? Well, you gather most of your club members, drive to a neutral course, with a higher degree of difficulty, and offer a distinct prize. Yes a serious competition. We played in the bucolic Sonoma Valley, an hour North of the City. It was a beautiful day, partly sunny, and temperatures in the mid-70s. The tree lined course was in remarkable shape. Excellent for scoring or not. The only noticeable distraction was the murders of crows inundating the idyllic environs. If they weren't thieving sandwiches from the carts, they would dance on the limbs above us cawing their hysterical laughter. Back to the prize if you please. The low four scores would form a 4-man team and compete against all the other NorCal teams, in Monterey, at the renowned Poppy Hills Golf Club. In case you are wondering, I did play rather well and fortunately qualified to be on the team. So I'm quite pleased.

Afterword

These musings are random, rambling, and varied. There is a thread which developed inadvertently. It has to do with balance, both mental and physical. The balance mentally is between aging and becoming weary, cynical and despairing — or aging with hope and joy aided by the unconditional love and influence of grandchildren. Physically, the balance is realizing activities taken for granted are no longer possible.

I'd like to add my early influences were the Beat writers. My literary landscape grew and expanded immensely. On that note I'd like to add a photo near and dear to my heart. My granddaughter Ashby is a good sport.

And the Beat goes on!

Made in the USA
Monee, IL
22 March 2023

30378284R00074